# Courts of Heaven Prayers for Your Children

**Pius Joseph © Text 2020**

**All rights Reserved.**

No part of this publication may be reproduced, distributed, or transmitted in any form or by any means, including photocopying, recording, or other electronic or mechanical methods, without the prior written permission of the publisher

Except in the case of brief quotations embodied in critical reviews and certain other noncommercial uses permitted by copyright law.

The author is aware that the application of this book may differ from one person to another as such things as faith, persistence, trust, and love for God can determine the outcomes that you receive from the application of the principles in this book.

Unless otherwise indicated, all scriptural quotations are taken from the King James Version © 1988-2007 Bible Soft Inc.

# TABLE OF CONTENTS

| | |
|---|---|
| TABLE OF CONTENTS | 3 |
| CHAPTER 1 | 1 |
| YOU'VE GOT TO KNOW | 1 |
| CHAPTER 2 | 7 |
| WHY PRAY THE COURTROOM PRAYER FOR YOUR CHILDREN | 7 |
| WHEN YOUR PRAYER HASN'T MADE THE CUT | 7 |
| THE SPEEDY INTERVENTION IN THE LIFE OF YOUR CHILDREN | 9 |

## CHAPTER 3           12

| | |
|---|---|
| HOW TO PRAY FOR YOUR CHILDREN IN THE COURTS OF HEAVEN | 12 |
| THE CREATION CAUSE | 13 |
| PURPOSE CAUSE | 19 |
| WORD CAUSE | 25 |
| GOD'S FAITHFULNESS CAUSE | 29 |

## CHAPTER 4           31

| | |
|---|---|
| HOW TO ACCESS THE COURTS OF HEAVEN FOR YOUR CHILDREN | 31 |
| MERCY AND THE BLOOD | 31 |
| DO UNTO OTHERS | 37 |
| THE PSALMS | 42 |
| THE UNENDING WORSHIP | 47 |

## CHAPTER 5           50

| | |
|---|---|
| RESTRAINING ORDERS AND INJUNCTIONS FOR YOUR CHILDREN | 50 |
| CATEGORISED INJUNCTIONS AND RESTRAINING ORDERS | 57 |
| FIRST CATEGORISED INJUNCTIONS, THE ATTACKED | 57 |
| SECOND CATEGORISED INJUNCTION | 58 |
| HE WOULD PROBABLY TRY | 59 |

## CHAPTER 6           64

| | |
|---|---|
| FREE THE BOUND | 64 |
| JUSTIFIED IMPRISONMENT | 65 |
| UNJUSTIFIABLE BOUNDS | 68 |

## CHAPTER 7     70

| | |
|---|---|
| COURTS OF HEAVEN PRAYERS FOR YOUR CHILDREN | 70 |
| INVITING THE HOLY SPIRIT | 71 |
| PRAYERS FOR DEALING WITH WAYWARDNESS | 75 |
| PRAYERS FOR AFFLICTION AND INFIRMITY | 79 |
| PRAYERS STRUGGLING IN LIFE AND SORROW | 86 |
| PRAYERS THAT BREAK GENERATIONAL CURSES | 89 |
| PRAYERS FOR THEIR HEDGE | 94 |
| PRAYERS FOR THEIR PURPOSE | 97 |
| RESTRAINING ORDERS AND INJUNCTIONS IN THE COURTS OF HEAVEN | 100 |
| PRAYERS FOR RELEASING THE CAPTIVE | 103 |
| IMPORTANT DECISION | 107 |
| MORE READING | 110 |

# CHAPTER 1

**You've got to Know**

In my little experience as a minister of the gospel, I have seen and heard about family stories that shook my spine. Some of the stories are too pitiable to be captured into the reality of print, and I may have to spend so much time before I explain them to you. The devil is aware that the family is one of the strongest structures used by God to bring forth men who will become great on the earth. Even Jesus who had a prophecy hanging over his head that he was going to bruise the head of the serpent, did not fall from the sky. He came from a family. Moses, the man who buried Pharaoh in the sea did not fall from the sky but proceeded from a family. Is it Elijah? Or David? Or even Samuel the prophet who was so prophetic that even his word did not fall to the ground. The family was their first launching pad. This explained the reason why when Jesus was born satan caused the execution of all children within a certain age to kill Jesus. The same thing he did when Moses was born. What was the target? The family!

All these biblical references above show the reason why the enemy is so focused on the family because he knows that great men and women arise from there. The devil is aware that whenever God wants to do damage to his works and kingdom, he raises a man and that man will come through the means of the family. Shortly before Jesus left the earth, he gave his disciples a very instructive charge that they were to begin preaching the gospel in Jerusalem, then Judaea, unto the uttermost parts of the earth.

Acts 1:8

> *But ye shall receive power, after that the Holy Ghost is come upon you: and ye shall be witnesses unto me both in Jerusalem, and in all Judaea, and in Samaria, and unto the uttermost part of the earth.*

The implication of the instruction that Jesus gave his disciples is simple, Jerusalem is the place where they were. It is like the family therefore, begin from there. Meaning that the family is the nucleus of any spiritual activity. Even Jesus knew that the family is the crux of the gospel which is why he gave his disciples the instruction to begin from Jerusalem. A man who has not made a definite impact on his family, cannot claim to conquer the whole world. The criteria for choosing a leader in the Bible is hinged on the family. He must be a husband of but one wife. One who rules his family well.

1 Timothy 3:2

> *A bishop then must be blameless, the husband of one wife, vigilant, sober, of good behaviour, given to hospitality, apt to teach;*

Don't be disturbed by Satan's search beam zeroed on your family. This isn't new and can never be strange. If Satan has been doing it before, he will still be doing the same thing again. That is why you see some families fight battles that have defied solutions. Grandad fought the same battle, fasted and prayed but he couldn't finish the battle even though he recorded some success. The same thing happened to the father and son. The battle seemed to weary the family, and they soon get used to it. They are simply tired and they can't do anything about it. Generation after generation of the same family, children continue to maintain an obstinate pattern of behaviour.

As we draw closer to the end of the age, Christians need to be aware that Satan is going to concentrate all of his Arsenal on the family unit. He knows that God has a great plan for raising a great army of people which will spring from different families across the earth. So he is paying very close attention to your family. What does he do? He attacks your children. You will begin to notice that your children are becoming obstinate and stubborn, often falling into the life of alcoholism and drugs. Even if Satan does not trap them with the above vices, they may be falling on the wrong side of the law all the time. Today they are restive, next tomorrow the prison. Even after serving a term, they still return to the life of evil and vices. And as a parent, you have become too tired to discuss it with anyone because of the way that your children are behaving. You have been looking at this attack from a very wrong perspective thinking that it is just something that your children will outgrow. But as you watched them growing, nothing has changed. This is to tell you that what your children are experiencing is not just a mere attack from the enemy. It is one that is centred on the family to cripple their spirituality and hinder what they will eventually become. Satan is not afraid of the kids. He is also not afraid of how beautiful they look. But what Satan fears so much is the future these children of yours have in God. So the devil started the battle very early on. Attacking them and encouraging them to do evil all the time. That is to tell you that this attack is coming straight from the pit of hell targeted towards your family and your children.

# CHAPTER 2

**Why pray the Courtroom Prayer for your Children**

**When your prayer hasn't made the cut**

Tired of seeing your children behave the way they have been behaving and you have done all sorts of prayer to no avail, then it is time to change your approach to praying so that answers can be guaranteed. Whenever you have prayed a particular prayer point for a prolonged period, and answers aren't coming, it is time to consider something different. What do you do? Consider taking the matter to the courts of heaven. Although we will consider this in details in the subsequent chapters of this book when we discuss the creation cause, I need to say here that Satan did not create your children, therefore, he has no right to interfere in what they should be. This is very essential when you are praying in the Courts of Heaven for the liberation of your children who are under the grip of the devil. If you see that the influence of the devil is much over the life of your children, then it may be time for you to take it to the Courts of Heaven for divine intervention.

Granted that you have been praying all this while and no result was imminent. The beauty of the courts of heaven prayer is that when you get there, something must happen on your behalf because you are asking God to rise as a judge and determine what you have brought before his courts. I encourage you to wipe all your tears because you are about to pray a prayer that is going to completely transform the life of your children. If you have been desiring them to be godly and to live according to the standards of what God has prescribed for all believers, then the courts of heaven prayer are your channel for making that a reality.

## The speedy intervention in the life of your children

Nothing brings a fast intervention in the life of your children like courts of heaven prayer. If there is the best way to pray, then I rather pray in the courts of God. When you pray in the courts of heaven, after the session God issues a decree or an order on your behalf. And since it is an order from God, it is quickly carried into effect by angels of the living God. Which is the reason why in courtroom prayer answers seem to be fast. One of the spiritual giants who have authored several books on the courtroom prayer was having a problem with one of his children that seemed to have defied all known solutions. He had prayed and nothing worked. He had also fasted and nothing worked. This prayer went on for many years until he decided to change his approach and took that child to the courts of heaven.

After praying in the Courts of Heaven for the deliverance of his child, just some few weeks later, the child was completely delivered from the stronghold of darkness. What took this man of God for several years to pray was handled in about 30 minutes. God simply issued an order against the demons that were attacking his child and that was it.

The above represents one of the powerful reasons why you should pray in the Courts of Heaven when dealing with the matters of your children. Besides the fact that praying in the Courts of Heaven on issues that bother their lifestyle or their destiny in God, it is the perfect will of God. The Bible makes us understand that he wants his will done in heaven as it is done on the earth. So when you pray in that manner, you are telling God that his will should be done concerning your children just as it is in heaven.

And I can tell you that God will gladly grant your request so that what he has destined them to be on the earth will be fulfilled.

# CHAPTER 3

## How to Pray for your Children in the Courts of Heaven

One of the critical instructions given in the book of James is for believers not to pray amiss. The fact that something is bothering you doesn't mean you will walk into the place of prayer and pray just the way you want to. Prayer is an art and mastering how to pray effectively is important in every courts of heaven prayer that we decided to engage. This account for the reason why so many believers are praying in the Courts of Heaven but are not seen any result.

James 4:3

> *Ye ask, and receive not, because ye ask amiss, that ye may consume it upon your lusts.*

In this chapter, I'm going to show you how to pray in the courts of heaven and plead the cause of your children and get answers.

## The Creation Cause

The Bible tells us in the book of Psalm that the earth is the Lord's and the fullness thereof.

Psalms 24:1

> *The earth is the Lord's, and the fulness thereof; the world, and they that dwell therein.*

Everything that you see on the earth was made and created by God. The devil has no hand in any creative work that you see around you. The Bible tells us in the book of John that by him were all things made and without him was nothing made. So God is the creator of the universe, and he can lay claim on all things that we see. The Bible tells us in the book of Genesis that when God wanted to create man, the godhead met and discussed the reality of creating a man in their image. And when that decision has been reached by the godhead, it was physically manifested on the earth in the book of Genesis 2:7:

> *And the Lord God formed man of the dust of the ground, and breathed into his nostrils the breath of life; and man became a living soul.*

Every human being was created by God. And all those who will subsequently be born and inhibit the earth, are going to be created by

God. The only difference is that they are following the command of God in the book of Genesis where he said that man should be fruitful, multiply, and replenish the face of the earth.

I must lay this foundation as this will help you plead your cause before the courts of heaven for your children. Having established that all the things that are created belong to God, how do you use this important fact of God's creation for your children in the courts of heaven?

The devil is an imitator, he does not create anything. All he does is to lay claim on the things that God has made. Even though he knew that God was the creator of the universe, he was still tempting Jesus to bow to him so that the same earth that Jesus created would be given to him. How absurd is this request of the devil?

Matthew 4:9

*Thy kingdom come. Thy will be done in earth, as it is in heaven.*

If the devil did not create your child, why is he laying claim to them? When God was creating man, the only three personalities that discussed that agenda before bringing it into reality is God the Father, God the Son, and God the Holy Spirit. Which is the reason why you hear the Bible says, let us make man in our image and after our likeness. Please, I want you to check that scripture critically whether you can find anywhere that God sought the opinion of the devil before creating man. If God didn't seek his opinion and man belong to God in entirety, then the devil has no claim at all to lay on the life of your children.

This is how to plead your cause in the courts of heaven for your children. Remember I told you, that it is not just praying in the Courts of heaven that brings result. It is an understanding of scriptural principles about the exclusive ownership of man by God that gives you the wisdom of pleading your cause before the courts of heaven and coming out with answers.

So if the devil does not want to leave your children alone, you can go to the courts of heaven and have him perpetually restrained from intermeddling into the affairs of your children. You can do that through a simple prayer in the courts of heaven in this manner:

*Holy Father, I thank you for the children that you have given to me. Thank you because you have said in your word that they are wonderfully made and fearfully created. This shows that you are the one who made them and have exclusive ownership of their lives. Therefore, Lord, I come before your Courts of Heaven on behalf of my children that the devil is trying to lay claim on their lives by making them behave in a wayward manner. Since the devil did not create them, he has no right to take total control over the lives of my children. I am asking you before your courts that a restraining order be issued against the devil and all his agents over what they are trying to do with the lives of my children in the name of Jesus.*

By praying in this manner, you are pleading the creation cause of your children before the courts of heaven. If God has the total ownership of your children, then why is the devil always interfering in the affairs of their lives? Not only is the devil interfering in the lives of your children, but he is also doing that in the household that has Christ as the head of the family.

Friends, the devil can continue to go all the way as long as he hasn't been rebuked. The moment you make him understand that he cannot proceed further with all this activity, he withdraws and leaves you alone. It is for this reason that the Bible says to resist the devil steadfastly, and he will flee from you. And this is what you do in the courts of heaven when the enemy is trying to control the lives of your children, ask if he was the one that created them.

I heard the testimony of a man whose child was severely sick. The man got angry and tired of the ill health that his child was suffering. One day, he brought out two chairs, one for God and the other for the devil. He started a conversation asking both who created the child. He would face one chair and say, if you didn't make the child then you don't have the right to attack him with sickness. After finishing that, his child was completely healed.

**Purpose Cause**

No human being on this earth ever came to the world empty. Every human being that you see on the face of the earth has a purpose for living. Which is the reason why you see some children become pastors, doctors, some become lawyers, and others become politicians, while some children will become scientists to solve some of the problems of men. And this has a biblical foundation too.

Matthew 25:14-19

> *For the kingdom of heaven is as a man travelling into a far country, who called his own servants, and delivered unto them his goods.*
> *15 And unto one he gave five talents, to another two, and to another one; to every man according to his several ability; and straightway took his journey.*
> *16 Then he that had received the five talents went and traded with the same, and made them other five talents.*

> *17 And likewise he that had received two, he also gained other two.*
> *18 But he that had received one went and digged in the earth, and hid his lord's money.*
> *19 After a long time the lord of those servants cometh, and reckoneth with them.*

The talent represents different potentials that God has deposited into every one of us. If you look at that scripture critically, nowhere was it written that the talent represents pastoral calling or something that has to do with ministry. It was just a simple talent that this master gave to each of his servants. It could be that one of the talents represent being a medical doctor. And that person is expected to use the medical talent to the glory of God. Through the medical practice of the doctor, he is expected to win souls for Christ and touch men for God.

From this, I believe you are beginning to see something new from the Scripture. That every child that is born into this world has a reason for living. He was created from eternity into our earthly realm to fulfil a divine purpose. And if the devil begins to mess up with anything in the life of your children that tempers with that divine purpose, you can use that creation purpose to plead your cause before the courts of heaven. And God will grant you your request because he is committed to the fulfilment of his plan on the earth. Which is the reason why the book of Matthew 6:10 says:

> *Thy kingdom come. Thy will be done in earth, as it is in heaven.*

Friends, a divine obligation has been placed upon you as a parent to be able to discover the purpose for which children were born into your family. While it is a good thing to rejoice at the birth of a newborn baby, your rejoicing should not stop there. It should also drive you to the place of prayer where you can know the divine plan and purpose of that child before the eyes of the Lord. If you do not know the plan and the purpose that God has for that child, how is it possible for you to plead the creation cause of that child before the courts of heaven? What if you are aware that the child is going to become a prophet with a great mantle for delivering people from the clutches of darkness, and you notice that the enemy is trying to tamper with the life of that child you can go before the courts of heaven and plead your cause. You can tell God that he didn't send your child to the earth for no reason. He sent this child to fulfil this particular purpose on earth. This is one of the greatest ways to pray for the fulfilment of the will of God in the lives of your children. When you come before the Lord to pray for his plans to be fulfilled on the earth, he is pleased.

Remember the Bible tells us in the book of Matthew when Jesus was teaching his disciples how to pray, he told them to pray that his will be done on earth as it is in heaven. Although there are a lot of misconceptions about this prayer because many during the church ages have been reciting it. That is a pattern of prayer and not the prayer in itself that needed to be recited all the times. God is telling us that we should start praying with Thanksgiving and end with Thanksgiving. It means any time that you pray, the prayer should be in that way.

This is one of the ways to end satanic disruptions in the lives of your children. Whatever God has created them for, tell it to him in the Courts of Heaven. The Bible tells us in the book of Philippians 1:6, that whatever God starts, he finishes it.

So if he started a beautiful thing in the life of your children, he is committed to completing that which he has started. And this is one of the things you can bring before the courts of heaven.

You can pray this prayer this way:

*Heavenly Father, I want to thank you for the lives of my children which you have graciously given to me. I thank you for the life of (mention the name of that child) and the great things you have promised to do with his life. Although I am not seeing that manifestation now, I trust you that you who have begun this good work of creating him and sending this child will complete that which you have started. I ask that let all the satanic interference in the life of my children be terminated today and may the purpose of which you have created them to live on the earth, be achieved in the name of Jesus.*

## Word Cause

There is something the word of God says about that your particular child in your family. You must open the word of God and know what he is saying about that child. The Bible tells us that children are heritage before the eyes of the Lord and happy is the man that has them full in his quiver. Again the same Bible tells us, that the angels of these little ones always behold the eyes of my father in heaven. There is a word for your child in the word of God. The only thing you have to do is to search and once you have found it, it can be the basis of your petition before the courts of heaven. Which is the reason why every believer who is minded to become courts of heaven prayer warrior must understand the word of God. It is through the word of God that you know what has been provided for you as a parent. It is based on the word of God that you know what God has stated concerning your children. It is via the word of God that you can understand that the devil does not have any right over the life of your children. What if you don't read the word? Then it will be impossible for you to know how to plead your word cause before the courts of heaven concerning the lives of your children.

Psalms 127:5

> *Happy is the man that hath his quiver full of them: they shall not be ashamed, but they shall speak with the enemies in the gate.*

Knowing what the word says will serve as an aid to pray effectively in the courts of heaven for your children. Your first duty and obligation right now are to find out what the word of God says concerning the lives of your children. As you know what the word says, you can lay all that scriptural truths before the courts of heaven and get answers for what you have been praying about.

I know that in our present world a lot of things are competing for our time. And if we are not careful, devoting quality time to the word of God can become a serious challenge.

The audio bible can never be a substitute for the word of God. But if you find yourself in a situation where reading the word is impossible, you can listen to the audio Bible.

You can pray in this way:

*Holy Father, you have said in your word that you know the plans you have for my children they are plans for good and not for evil to give them an expected end. I know through the infallibility of your word that it is settled in all realms. Therefore, I pray today that the power of the Scripture be activated over the lives of my children and let them live to fulfil the very reason for their creation in the name of Jesus.*

Even if your child is suffering from an affliction, it is the same way you are going to pray to handle it. What did the word of God say concerning your child? When you have found it, take that particular Scripture to the courts of heaven and plead your cause.

## God's Faithfulness Cause

While men are variable unless the Holy Spirit helps us to be faithful to God all the times, God is not. David had a splendid walk with the Lord and through the inspiration of the Holy Spirit, he was able to write the following words in the book of Psalms I have never seen the righteous forsaken or beg for bread.

Hebrews 13:8

> *Jesus Christ the same yesterday, and to day, and for ever.*

The same God who walked with Abraham, Moses, David, Paul the apostle, Peter, James, and John is the same God that we serve. He never changes. Even though man may change, God does not. He is committed to bringing to pass all that he has said concerning your life or the promises he has spoken over the lives of your children. Which is the reason why sometimes when you have forgotten the things that God has promised you, he reminds you about them.

One of the reasons why a believer can trust God is because God is faithful. He does not break his promises. Even if the words that came out of the mouth of God were to be mistakes, in faithfulness he will fulfil those words. And when you come before the courts of heaven this is one of the things you can plead over the lives of your children. The faithfulness of God.

Although this is closely associated with some of the things we have discussed above, it can be relied on during courts of heaven prayer.

# CHAPTER 4

## How to Access the Courts of Heaven for your Children

### Mercy and the Blood

1 John 1:9

> *If we confess our sins, he is faithful and just to forgive us our sins, and to cleanse us from all unrighteousness.*

Speaks volume about the mercy of God. The first thing you need to do is to clear out everything that can stop your courts of heaven prayers for your children. The person coming before the throne of God must thoroughly wash his garment in the mercy of God. If that is not done, the courts of heaven prayer will only amount to a waste of time. The reason why you should ask for mercy is because there are things that you might have done that are standing against you before God. And Satan can accuse you before God as he did to Joshua the High priest. He resisted him until mercy was shown to Joshua. First, cleanse yourself from anything that is wrong and if you feel that you haven't done anything wrong, you should still ask for mercy because there are sins of commission or sins of omissions too.

There is nothing that puts you away from the Courts of Heaven like sin and iniquity. The Bible tells us in the book of Habakkuk, that the eyes of the Lord are too holy to behold iniquity:

Habakkuk 1:13

> *Thou art of purer eyes than to behold evil, and canst not look on iniquity: wherefore lookest thou upon them that deal treacherously, and holdest thy tongue when the wicked devoureth the man that is more righteous than he?*

If the eyes of the Lord are too holy to behold iniquity, is it possible for that same iniquity to come into his courts where he administers the affairs of eternity and mortality? Of course, not.

As mighty as the love that God has for Adam and Eve when they decided to embrace iniquity and sin, he stopped visiting them in the cool of the evening in the Garden of Eden.

Isaiah 59:1-2

> *Behold, the Lord's hand is not shortened, that it cannot save; neither his ear heavy, that it cannot hear:*
> *2 But your iniquities have separated between you and your God, and your sins have hid his face from you, that he will not hear.*

It was the same sin that serves as a termination of their stay in the Garden of Eden.

Psalms 24:3-4

> *Who shall ascend into the hill of the Lord? or who shall stand in his holy place?*
> *4 He that hath clean hands, and a pure heart; who hath not lifted up his soul unto vanity, nor sworn deceitfully.*

The Bible tells us in the book of Psalms that who can ascend into his holy hills. In the subsequent verses, an answer was provided. That it is only him that has clean hands who has not lifted his hands to vanity. If a man has not embraced the way of sin and iniquity, he can enter into the Courts of heaven.

Does that mean that anyone who has sinned or done anything wrong cannot enter into the Courts of Heaven? Well, if a believer will subject himself to the washing power of the blood of Jesus, he can still enter into the Courts of Heaven and offer his prayers there. The Bible tells us that the blood of Jesus cleanses us from all sins. The number one step for gaining access into the Courts of Heaven is to submit yourself to the cleansing power of the blood of Jesus. You plead the blood of Jesus upon your life and apply its cleansing power to your body, soul, and spirit. Once you have been washed by the blood of Jesus, your courts of heaven prayer will be offered without hindrance.

The failure to submit yourself to the washing power of the blood of Jesus will hinder the effectiveness of your courts of heaven prayer. Sin or iniquity is what separates man and God. Whenever God sees sin, he distances himself. Whenever God sees purity, he draws himself closer.

One of the greatest tools that God has left for us on the earth to continue to help us unite with God even when we have fallen short of his glory, is the blood of Jesus. It doesn't matter the type of sin that you have committed once you can bring yourself under the washing power of the blood of Jesus. It will cleanse you and remove any hindrance that can prevent your courts of heaven prayer from being effective. Never forget that before you begin to do any prayer in the Courts of heaven, bring yourself under the washing power of the blood of Jesus

Hebrews 10:19

> *Having therefore, brethren, boldness to enter into the holiest by the blood of Jesus,*

**Do Unto Others**

The next step that you need to take after pleading the blood of Jesus is to release it. If you cannot forgive others for the wrong that they have done to you, God cannot forgive you. It is that simple, and we don't need to form any formula around it.

Matthew 6:12

> *And forgive us our debts, as we forgive our debtors.*

You want God to forgive you, then forgive those who have offended you. Pleading the blood of Jesus to gain access to the courts of heaven without forgiving or releasing those who have offended is useless.

As we forgive others their wrongs, that is how God can forgive us our wrong too.

Which is the reason why the Bible says, forgive us our debts as we forgive those who trespass against us. If you have received forgiveness from God, you also have to give forgiveness to others. That is how it is.

Matthew 18:23-35

> *Therefore is the kingdom of heaven likened unto a certain king, which would take account of his servants.*
> *24 And when he had begun to reckon, one was brought unto him, which owed him ten thousand talents.*
> *25 But forasmuch as he had not to pay, his lord commanded him to be sold, and his wife, and children, and all that he had, and payment to be made.*
> *26 The servant therefore fell down, and worshipped him,*

*saying, Lord, have patience with me, and I will pay thee all.*

*27 Then the lord of that servant was moved with compassion, and loosed him, and forgave him the debt.*

*28 But the same servant went out, and found one of his fellowservants, which owed him an hundred pence: and he laid hands on him, and took him by the throat, saying, Pay me that thou owest.*

*29 And his fellowservant fell down at his feet, and besought him, saying, Have patience with me, and I will pay thee all.*

*30 And he would not: but went and cast him into prison, till he should pay the debt.*

*31 So when his fellowservants saw what was done, they were very sorry, and came and told unto their lord all that was done.*

*32 Then his lord, after that he had called him, said unto him, O thou wicked servant, I forgave thee all that debt, because thou desiredst me:*

*33 Shouldest not thou also have had compassion on thy fellowservant, even as I had pity on thee?*

*34 And his lord was wroth, and delivered him to the tormentors, till he should pay all that was due unto him.*

*35 So likewise shall my heavenly Father do also unto you, if ye from your hearts forgive not every one his brother their trespasses.*

This Scripture is self-explanatory and nothing more needs to be said about it. The master forgave this man his debt but the same man did not have the heart to forgive others.

That is a principle of God. We have committed several wrongs and errors against him. He forgave us. And someone did something small to us, and we don't want to let go. As long as we don't let go, our initial offences before God are remembered. Be it fornication, theft, lust, et cetera. That is the only circumstances in the Bible that God remembers our sin. If we do not forgive others, we bring to his remembrance all the things that we have done in the past.

As you are reading this right now, there are people that you know you need to forgive. They indeed did what badly hurt you. It is also true that what they did in your eyes was big. But you have to release forgiveness if praying in the Courts of Heaven is what you want to do now. And I know that the Holy Spirit is beginning to nudge your heart concerning people that you need to forgive. Do so quickly so that you can have access to the Courts of Heaven for your prayers. If you do not forgive, you will waste your time in the courts of heaven and no order will be given against the devil or his agents.

**The Psalms**

Psalm 100:4

> *Enter into his gates with thanksgiving, and into his courts with praise: be thankful unto him, and bless his name.*

The Scripture under reference tells us to enter into his gates with thanksgiving and into his courts with praise. There are two things you need to do to gain access into the courts of heaven where our courtroom prayers are going to be offered.

A. Thanksgiving – What will give you access to the gates of heaven is Thanksgiving. And there are several things to be thankful to God for. One of which is the gift of life. The air you breathe freely is being paid by some people as oxygen in the hospital. The salvation you have was given to you by Jesus Christ even though there are some people that you know who perished without knowing Jesus. The financial provision that you have been enjoying can constitute a serious focus of your thanksgiving. The health of your family that no one has fallen sick in the past year or six months, is also something that you can be thankful to God for. What is it? If you can only think deeply about the things that God has been doing for you, you will be very thankful to him. These are some of the factors that can constitute the focus of your praise to gain access to the courts of heaven. If your destination is the courts of heaven, then Thanksgiving must be your starting point. You start by thanking God for all he has done for you. Anything at all that you can remember that God has done for you in the past or the present, use it to thank God. The moment you begin to thank God and you do it effectively, the gates of heaven will be opened to you. If you are travelling to British Columbia, Canada and you decided to stop at Washington State, will you say in all honesty that you went to British Columbia? I believe, no! Your journey will be seen as completed when you have arrived in British Columbia, Canada. Your Thanksgiving is the same as the example above. Thanksgiving will take you to the gates of heaven but won't grant you access into the courts of heaven for your prayers. To be able to gain access to the courts of heaven, you need another different step that you need to take. I will show you the next step.

B. Praise – This is the tool that takes you beyond the limits of the gates of heaven into the Courts of Heaven where your courtroom prayer is going to be carried out. After you have thanked God with the whole of your heart, the next important thing that you must do is to offer praises to God. It is your praises that will usher you into the Courts of heaven for you to begin your prayers. This step is very necessary for you to follow carefully so that you can arrive at the desired destination of the Courts of Heaven. In case you don't know what to praise God for, let me give you a small list of what can constitute the subject of your praise.

a. Praise God for being your saviour.
b. Praise God for the demonstration of his might in your life.

c. Praise God for the demonstration of his might and power in the lives of others.
d. Praise God for his faithfulness in your life.
e. Praise God for being your creator.
f. Praise God for being the creator of the universe.
g. Praise God for the things he has created which you can see.
h. Praise God for the sufficiency of his power at work on the earth.
i. Praise God for the demonstration of his might which you have seen in the Scriptures.
j. Praise God for the promises, prophecies, and every word that he has spoken over your life either personally by the revelation which you have received or through a prophet of the Lord.

These are things you can use to praise God for if you don't know what to use as the focus of your praise. The careful observance of this protocol of the Psalms will take you from the gates into the courts of heaven for your prayers.

## The unending Worship

One of the powerful things that take place continuously in the courts of God is worship.

Revelation 4:8-11

> *And the four beasts had each of them six wings about him; and they were full of eyes within: and they rest not day and night, saying, Holy, holy, holy, Lord God Almighty, which was, and is, and is to come.*
>
> *9 And when those beasts give glory and honour and thanks to him that sat on the throne, who liveth for ever and ever,*

> *10 The four and twenty elders fall down before him that sat on the throne, and worship him that liveth for ever and ever, and cast their crowns before the throne, saying,*
> *11 Thou art worthy, O Lord, to receive glory and honour and power: for thou hast created all things, and for thy pleasure they are and were created.*

The Scripture above tells us that the four beasts rest not day and night. They are before the courts of God and one of the things that takes place there is constant worship. After you have pleaded the blood of Jesus, forgiven others, observed the protocols of the Psalms, the next thing to do after you have gained entrance into the courts of heaven is to worship. There is no place you can't enter in this life if you understand the rules, procedures, and protocols there. If you want to enter into the White House, there are procedures and protocols which you need to follow. If you follow them, you will enter the White House. If you refuse to follow them, you will never find yourself there. It is possible that before you see the president of the United States of America in the White House, you may need to book an appointment. Even with your appointment, there are things you need to do when you get to the White House before you can see Mr President. From the booking of your appointment down to the procedures you need to follow to enter into the White House, all of these can be categorised as steps you need to take or the protocols to observe to gain entrance into the White House. This is also true for the courts of heaven prayer. All that we have outlined so far are the steps you need to take before you gain access into the Courts of heaven. And even when you gain access into the Courts of heaven, you still need to offer worship to God for you to offer your prayers in the courts.

# CHAPTER 5

## Restraining Orders and Injunctions for Your Children

1 Samuel 7:13

> *So the Philistines were subdued, and they came no more into the coast of Israel: and the hand of the Lord was against the Philistines all the days of Samuel.*

Whenever we speak about injunctions and restraining orders that are permanent, some people will be thinking that it is impossible to have such level of victory against the devil. When it comes to the word of God, my opinion and yours are not relevant what matters is the word of God. Once the word is emphatic about anything, we have no choice but to follow what the word says. We must discard our opinion and align what we think with the word of God.

Mark 9:25

> *When Jesus saw that the people came running together, he rebuked the foul spirit, saying unto him, Thou dumb and deaf spirit, I charge thee, come out of him, and enter no more into him.*

Teaches us an important lesson that the devil can be bound forever in certain areas of our lives. That was the reason why when Jesus was casting out that devil out of the life of that boy, he said to enter into him no more. In effect, an injunction and a restraining order were issued against that demon, for you, it is settled forever. Don't ever come around the life of this one anymore because you have been ordered and you are commanded to obey the thing that I have told you to do. How wonderful to have a good understanding of the word of God and enforce that victory in the courts of heaven for your children.

In your personal life, you will recall that there are victories that you have won against the devil in certain areas of your life that the enemy has never bothered you any longer about that issue. Why? The victory was so commanding, and the devil knows that he has been comprehensively beaten that his power to make noise again has been taken. It was to him like what happened in the book of 1 Samuel 7:23, *so the Philistines were subdued that they came no more into the coast of Israel.*

Let me give you an example. When I first became a Christian, I was battling with a particular thought pattern. Anytime someone walked close to me, I would hear this condemning thought in my heart that sounded like me. It would say, just look at the legs of this person they looked ugly. This continued for a while until one day I opened up to a brother in Christ Jesus, who told me that the Bible says people are wonderfully made and fearfully created. I felt that I needed to do something about this train of thought I was gradually accepting in my life. I did not even bother to go and check the word of God whether it was true or not. Armed with the phrases of those scriptures, I took the battle to the gates of hell. Whenever that thought came flying, I would say wonderfully made and fearfully created. Whenever my eyes cast on the legs of someone or eyes, as the devil used to do with me then, I would quote that scripture quickly in my heart even before the thought came. I was very young in Christ at that time and so many of the truths of scripture that I know now, I didn't know them that time. The strange thing is that the devil was so beaten badly by what I was doing that he came no more into my coast to bother me with his wicked thoughts. I didn't even know when I defeated that thought. I just realised that the thought had gone. What happened? A onetime defeat.

And if I begin to interview so many believers now about some of the great victories that they have recorded in their lives, it will be recorded after record of deliverance that the devil has never been able to gainsay or resist. They will tell you, I used to struggle with this and that but now, no more. And since so so so years that it stopped, it has never happened again.

Friends, I want something to enter your head and let the mind of your understanding be opened to the truth of the word of God that injunctions and restraining orders against the devil forbidding him from acting or doing some things in the lives of your children is possible. And this teaching is not just a fable or babbling. It takes its root deep in the scripture and the word of God.

John 8:36

John 8:36

> *If the Son therefore shall make you free, ye shall be free indeed.*

The word indeed as used in the scripture referenced above shows that freedom is without any conditions attached to it. Once the Son of man, Jesus, gives you victory either by the word of God or the inspiration of the Holy Spirit, nothing shall be able to stop it. That freedom is guaranteed and the devil can't do anything about it. How beautiful, isn't it?

Nahum 1:9

*What do ye imagine against the Lord? he will make an utter end: affliction shall not rise up the second time.*

I want you to read this scripture very well before you look at what I am about to say to you. I will make an utter end. Did you hear what the Lord said, I will make a complete end of the affliction, the attack of the devil on your children, the trap of bad lifestyles that he has placed for your children, the Lord said I will end. And after I have ended it, I won't stop there. There are other things that I will do for your children. That affliction, the attack, the works of satan, I will give you this victory that the affliction is not permitted to rise again the second time. It is not permitted to come again. As it has gone. It has gone forever. It will no longer come into your coast. Are you seeing that the scriptures made it possible for us to have total victories against the works of the devil through the finished works of Christ Jesus forever? How amazing!

## Categorised injunctions and Restraining Orders

I will be speaking to two categories of persons here, those whose children are under the attack of the devil and those whose children haven't been touched by the enemy yet. Now, before you shout and say, brother Pius, nothing is gonna happen to my kids, let me tell you that I will be surprised to hear that the devil has not started planning something against your children already. What do you need to do, prevent the devil even before he started operating against your life and children now.

## First Categorised Injunctions, the Attacked

There is always hope for the righteous if your children are already under the heavy barrage of satanic and demonic gunfire, and you are concerned that they have been hit by what the enemy has been doing, you can do something about that. All hope is not lost, you can issue a restraining order from the courts of heaven against the devil to leave your children alone. You will do this through the power of prayer and it will be done. You present your petition before the courts of heaven with justifiable reasons why the devil should be restrained with finality. If the Lord grants your request against the works of the devil, he would stop, and it will surprise you the sudden changes that will begin to happen in the lives of your children.

## Second Categorised injunction

The second case refers to people whose children are doing okay but decided to fold their hands across their chest. They are now at ease in Zion believing nothing would happen. Unfortunately, many believers are in this category. They have forgotten that the mission statement of the devil as captured in the Book of John 10:10 is to steal, kill and destroy. Am I trying to make you afraid of the devil, certainly no! You don't have to be afraid of someone that the Bible says, the Lord (Father of Jesus), said to our Lord (Jesus), seat at my right hand until I make your enemies your footstool. That is, all the devils and demons! It is on their heads that the Lord Jesus Christ rest his footstool.

However, the best time to prepare for war, as it is often said, is at the time of peace! Now that the devil hasn't done anything to your children yet, you need to go to the courts of heaven and get an injunctive order against the devil so that he would be permanently bound.

## He Would Probably Try

An injunctive or restraining order is permanent against the works of the devil. But the fact that you got an order of restraint against the devil doesn't mean that he won't try to contempt it. This is where many believers miss it in life and victory. When they saw victory, they will rejoice and say, aha, the Lord has done it. The devil goes his way and one day returns to show them the signs of what they believe that they have gotten the victory over. They throw the victory away and return to the same situation.

There is nowhere in the word of God that the Lord directed us to go and fight the devil. We don't need to fight him. Jesus has already fought him and defeated him. The only thing left for us to do is to continue to remind the devil of his defeat through the word of God.

Colossians 2:14-15

> *Blotting out the handwriting of ordinances that was against us, which was contrary to us, and took it out of the way, nailing it to his cross;*

*15 And having spoiled principalities and powers, he made a shew of them openly, triumphing over them in it.*

I want you to know that after you have gotten the victory in the courts of heaven against the devil, he would come to you again to try and see if he can contempt the order that God has given against him by bringing signs of the same thing. For instance, you have prayed and gotten a restraining order in the courts of heaven against the spirit of infirmity that has been tormenting your children. After you have come out from the courts of heaven, everything disappears and then after six months, the symptoms returned. What you do is to remind that lying devil that there is already an injunction or order restraining him from the body of this child of yours and by that same order of injunction, he is commanded to depart in Jesus name. What are you doing? You are reminding the devil of the victory you had received through the blood of Jesus, and the courts of heaven. As a result, he isn't permitted to come and temper with the life of your child anymore.

In law, this is done most of the times whenever a plaintiff (the person that went to court), gets a judgment against another person (Defendant). If in the judgment, the court restrained the defendant against whom the judgment was delivered not to temper with the subject matter, for instance, land, and he does. The plaintiff will first of all remind him that there is already a subsisting judgment of the court along with an order restraining him from going into the land.

The example above is the same thing that happens to the devil when he comes back after you have gone to the courts of heaven and obtained a restraining order against him. When he comes back, remind him of what the Lord has done through the courts of heaven prayers and point him to scriptural truth that confirmed your victory.

# CHAPTER 6

**Free the Bound**

Isaiah 49:24-25

> *Shall the prey be taken from the mighty, or the lawful captive delivered?*
> *25 But thus saith the Lord, Even the captives of the mighty shall be taken away, and the prey of the terrible shall be delivered: for I will contend with him that*

> *contendeth with thee, and I will save thy children.*

This particular prayer will be useful for those whose children are currently in prison. If your children have been sent to jail, they can be released through courts of heaven prayers. This particular session isn't about children alone, once you have anyone that you have fathered or mothered as a parent or guardian, you can pray for them in the courts of heaven and God will hear.

## Justified Imprisonment

When someone has done something wrong, and he got sent to jail, then there is a justified reason for his imprisonment. He did evil and the long hand of the law caught him. If you don't know the protocol and you just go into the courts of heaven to pray, it will not be answered.

The way to pray this courts of heaven prayer is to come before the Lord acknowledging the wrong of your children and pleading to God for him to show mercy because they did what is wrong.

Luke 23:39-43

> *And one of the malefactors which were hanged railed on him, saying, If thou be Christ, save thyself and us.*
>
> *40 But the other answering rebuked him, saying, Dost not thou fear God, seeing thou art in the same condemnation?*
>
> *41 And we indeed justly; for we receive the due reward of our deeds: but this man hath done nothing amiss.*
>
> *42 And he said unto Jesus, Lord, remember me when*

> *thou comest into thy kingdom.*
> *43 And Jesus said unto him, Verily I say unto thee, To day shalt thou be with me in paradise.*

Look at what this other guy on the cross with Jesus said. He recognized his fault, agreed that what he has done was wrong and duly deserved to be punished, but also pleaded to God for mercy. He was simply saying, Jesus indeed I know what I have done is wrong against the law and this punishment, I did deserve it. When Jesus saw the remorseful way in which he presented his request, he was forgiven and then granted access to paradise. Many will think, but this man did not say the sinners' prayers or something like that. The most important thing is believing. Salvation is believing first in the heart.

Many have been confessing but don't believe in the heart and their state remains the way it has been. But by openly declaring that Jesus is innocent of what the Pharisees and the Sadducees accuse him of, to me this sounds like confessing that Jesus is Lord following Romans 10:9-10.

Romans 9:15

> *For he saith to Moses, I will have mercy on whom I will have mercy, and I will have compassion on whom I will have compassion.*

From these two scriptures, God can show mercy to whoever that he desires and that is what you need to have when you go into the courts of heaven for your prayers for your children who are in jail.

## Unjustifiable Bounds

There are injustices in our societies and sometimes innocent people can be thrown in jail even when they never committed that offence that was alleged against them. That is the kind of world that we live in where people love to do wickedness against others. If you are sure that child or children are innocent of the accusation for which they were jailed, you can go to the courts of heaven and pray for their release. You tell God that to judge by the standard of his word whether it is right for your children to be in jail for an offence that they never committed. And if by the standard of his word that they aren't supposed to be in prison, then he should release them. As you pray this prayer in the courts of heaven, I want you to have this understanding that the hearts of kings is in the hand of the Lord, and he turns it in whichever direction that he desires. God can cause anyone to have them released, and I pray that it shall be your portion as you go to the courts of heaven in the name of Jesus.

# CHAPTER 7

**Courts of Heaven Prayers for your Children**

Before you commence the prayer in this chapter, you need to follow the procedures for gaining access to the courts of heaven. For our prayers, I will summarise the procedures as follows:

1. Plead for mercy

2. Plead the blood of Jesus over your life

3. Offer forgiveness to others who have sinned against you.

4. Follow the procedure of the Psalms to get access into the courts of heaven by Thanksgiving and praise (see Psalms 100:4)

5. Offer worship in the Courts of Heaven for effective courtroom prayer.

**Inviting the Holy Spirit**

One of the ministries of the Holy Spirit is to help the believer to pray in the will of God.

Romans 8:26-27

> *Likewise the Spirit also helpeth our infirmities: for we know not what we should pray for as we ought: but the Spirit itself maketh intercession for us with groanings which cannot be uttered.*
> *27 And he that searcheth the hearts knoweth what is the mind of the Spirit, because he maketh intercession for*

> *the saints according to the will of God.*

A believer who wants to pray in the perfect will of God must learn to work with the Holy Spirit. The Scriptural reference we have just seen said we don't know how to pray as we are supposed to but the Holy Spirit helps us to pray and makes intercession for us according to the will of God. From experience, I have never seen any successful courts of heaven prayer that I have prayed in my life or with a group of friends without the help of the Holy Spirit. He is the perfect courts of heaven prayer master that you will need when you get to the courts of heaven. If you ignore his ministry in this area of your life, it is possible not to pray effectively as you ought to.

The Holy Spirit will help you to present your case in the proper way that you are supposed to before the courts of heaven. Remember what the Scripture says, that he helps us to pray the perfect will of God. So before you begin your prayers in the courts of Heaven for your children, the one personality you should invite is the Holy Spirit. And that is what we are going to be doing right now.

**Reflection**

John 14:26

> *But the Comforter, which is the Holy Ghost, whom the Father will send in my name, he shall teach you all things, and bring all things to your remembrance, whatsoever I have said unto you.*

John 16:13

> *Howbeit when he, the Spirit of truth, is come, he will guide you into all truth: for he shall not speak of himself; but whatsoever he shall hear, that shall he speak:*

*and he will shew you things to come.*

Holy Father, thank you for the privilege that you have given to me to come before the courts of heaven right now to you be all the glory and honour in the name of Jesus.

Heavenly Father, you have said in your word that when the spirit of truth is come, the Holy Spirit, he will guide me into all truth. I pray for the guidance of the Holy Spirit in this Courts of Heaven prayers for my children in the name of Jesus.

Righteous Father, I invite the presence of the Holy Spirit into this prayer in the Courts of Heaven in the name of Jesus.

Gracious Father, I make demands for the intercessory ministry of the Holy Spirit to be active from the beginning of this courts of heaven prayer for my children to the end in the name of Jesus.

Thank You Holy Father, for the presence of the Holy Spirit in this Courts of Heaven prayers for my children to you be all the glory and honour in the name of Jesus.

## Prayers for Dealing with Waywardness

One of the greatest attacks of the enemy is to make your children wayward. So that every time you look at your children, you are grieved in your heart. In the same way that Esau became a pain to Jacob and Rachel, that is one of the ways that the enemy wants to use to attack your children. That was the same attack that he brought upon the life of the sons of Eli. Every day of his life, whenever he looks at his children, it was a pain to him. It got to a point that the same children that came from his loins became the reason why the old man, Eli was buried before his time. This was an attack of the enemy upon the lives of the children of this man of God. When anybody wants to refer to the children of Eli, the Bible says they were sons of Belial because they knew not the Lord. I pray that that should not be your portion because you are not permitted to bring children to the earth who will become a pain to you in the name of Jesus.

**Reflection**

Psalms 127:5

> *Happy is the man that hath his quiver full of them: they shall not be ashamed, but they shall speak with the enemies in the gate.*

Proverbs 22:6

> *Train up a child in the way he should go: and when he is old, he will not depart from it.*

Holy Father, I come before you to present my petition before your courts. I know by your word that I am not supposed to bring forth children whose life will become a source of pain to me. However, you can see the kind of lifestyle that my children are living in. They are no longer subject to my authority and the spirit of rebellion has taken over their life. I make demands before your courts that let the spirit of rebellion that has taken hold of the life of my children to be judged in the name of Jesus.

Holy Father, you have said in your word that the generation of the righteous shall be blessed. It is a blessing that you have ordained for my children not a lifestyle of rebellion. I stand before your courts and I ask that a restraining order be issued against the spirit of rebellion that has come upon my children in the name of Jesus.

Gracious Father, in the same way, that Jesus did not come to the earth to become a pain to his parents, Mary and Joseph. I make demands that my children shall not become a source of pain to me in the name of Jesus.

Righteous Father, whatever trap of rebellion that the enemy has set over the life of my children to make them lead a wayward life, let the snares be destroyed by the power in the name of Jesus.

Holy Father, I pray that from the courts of heaven right now you will release your fire that will consume all forms of stubbornness from the life of my children in the name of Jesus.

Righteous Father, it is not in accordance with your will for me to bring forth for trouble. I will not give birth to children that will continue to bring trouble to my life. I pray that my seed shall live according to what you have ordained for them in the name of Jesus.

Holy Father, whatever arrow of waywardness that the enemy has fired into the life of my children, I send that arrow back to where it came from in the name of Jesus.

Gracious Father, every kind of pressure that the enemy is using the friends of my children to make them live a life that is not according to the word of God and what I have taught them, I disconnect them from such association in the name of Jesus.

Thank You Holy Father, for hearing me in Jesus name.

## Prayers for Affliction and infirmity

Infirmity is a spirit and one of the greatest attacks that the enemy can throw into the lives of your children is the spirit of infirmity and sickness. This is in two categories. Your children may not be suffering from any infirmity at the moment but that does not mean that the enemy is not planning to fire such an arrow into their lives. And you can be faster than the enemy by acting even before he sends those arrows into the lives of your children in the future. When God was speaking to the King of Assyria, he said he will not shoot any arrow in the city.

2 Kings 19:32

> *Therefore thus saith the Lord concerning the king of Assyria, He shall not come into this city, nor shoot an arrow there, nor come before it with shield, nor cast a bank against it.*

Look at that Scripture, he will not shoot any arrow in this city means that God is trying to prevent him from doing something in the future.

However, if your children are already suffering from the spirit of infirmity released by the devil into the lives of your children, you can ask God for healing and bind the spirit of infirmity in the Courts of Heaven. The Bible says I am the God your healer and I will put none of these diseases which I brought upon the Egyptians (Exodus 15:26). It is the will of God that we should prosper in all realms of life – both in health and in life.

And when the devil is attacking your children with the spirit of infirmity or sickness, you are not prospering in health according to what the word of God has said.

What do you need to do? Go into the Courts of Heaven and have the spirit of infirmity restrained from ever attacking your children. We have already seen from scriptural basis that it is possible to have total and complete victory against the works of the devil, including the spirit of infirmity.

In the Courts of heaven at this moment, you are going to pray prayers that will kick the spirit of infirmity out of the life of your children. And if your children are enjoying good health, affirm that by the truth of the word of God so that they can continue to be healthy.

**Reflection**

3 John 2

> *Beloved, I wish above all things that thou mayest prosper and be in health, even as thy soul prospereth.*

Malachi 4:2

> *But unto you that fear my name shall the Sun of righteousness arise with healing in his wings; and ye shall go forth, and grow up as calves of the stall.*

Holy Father, I want to thank you for the promise of your word that you have declared that you are the God our healer. I bring this child of mine (mention the name of that particular child who is currently suffering from the spirit of infirmity) before your courts at this moment. I am asking you to judge based on the standard of your word whether it is permissible for my child to continue to suffer from this affliction since your word has already said that you took our infirmities. If you find by the standard of your word that my petition is justifiable according to the Scriptures, then let my child (mention the name of that child that is suffering from the spirit of infirmity) be healed right now in the name of Jesus.

Holy Father, you have said in your word that the Son of righteousness shall arise with healing in his wings. I make demands that you will arise with healings in your wings and cause the manifestation of that healing on the life of my (mention the name of the child that is suffering from the spirit of infirmity) now in the name of Jesus.

Glorious Father, it is the justice of your courts that one man shall not bear the sin or iniquity of another person. If it is as a result of our sins as parents that have opened the door for the devil to bring the spirit of infirmity into the life of our children, I ask you to judge by the standard of your word that these children have done nothing wrong. And if you find according to the standard of your word in the book of Ezekiel that every man shall die for his sins, then let the spirit of infirmity that has come upon the life of my children be judged before your courts and let that spirit depart from the life of my children in the name of Jesus.

Holy Father, every symptom that is associated with this infirmity that is currently in the life of my children I ask that let that symptom be gone in the name of Jesus.

Heavenly Father, you have decreed in your word that you will make an utter end of the works of darkness against the life of my children. You further said that affliction shall not arise again the second time. Now that my children have been healed of this infirmity it will never return into their lives again in the name of Jesus.

Glorious Father, anything that wants to physically hinder the manifestation of that healing in the lives of my children, let that limitation be taken away before your courts in the name of Jesus.

Righteous Father, you have said in your word that he that the Father has set free, that person is free indeed. From today I decree the complete freedom of my children from the grip of affliction and infirmities in the name of Jesus.

Heavenly Father, whatever spirit of infirmity that the enemy intends to release into the lives of my children in the future that spirit is arrested and restrained from operating in the lives of my children in the name of Jesus.

Holy Father, let the fire of the Holy Spirit consume every snare of infirmity that the enemy has planned against the life of my children to manifest in the future in the name of Jesus.

Righteous Father, I bring my children under the protection of the blood of Jesus, and I shield them from every spirit of infirmity that the enemy wants to release into their lives in the name of Jesus.

Thank You Holy Father because this is the confidence I have in you whenever I bring any petition before your courts you hear and answer. In the name of Jesus, amen.

**Prayers Struggling in life and Sorrow**

Have you ever seen people whose life is constantly in sorrow and struggling all the time? Often, this is an attack of the enemy upon the life of those people. And if a restraining order isn't issued against what the enemy intends to do, you can begin to see that your children are struggling in life. This is one prayer that as a parent you should endeavour to pray for the life of your children.

This is not to say that your children will not experience challenges in life. But there is a huge difference between challenges and constant life of struggling and sorrow.

## Reflection

1 John 5:14-15

> *And this is the confidence that we have in him, that, if we ask any thing according to his will, he heareth us:*
> *15 And if we know that he hear us, whatsoever we ask, we know that we have the petitions that we desired of him.*

Isaiah 7:7

> *Thus saith the Lord God, It shall not stand, neither shall it come to pass.*

Holy Father, I thank you for the life of my children because of the promise you have for their lives, and I know that you will be glorified in every dimension of their lives in the name of Jesus.

Heavenly Father, whatever sorrow that the enemy has attached to the lives of my children today it is destroyed before your courts in the name of Jesus.

Gracious Father, you have said in your word that you wished above all things that we should prosper in all realms of our existence on the earth. I commit my children before your throne that their lives will not be marked by struggling in the name of Jesus.

Righteous Father, every spirit of hardship that the enemy intends to send into the lives of my children, I ask for the issuance of a permanent restraining order against that spirit right now before your courts in the name of Jesus.

Holy Father, let your judgemental fire be released from your courts to consume all the plans of the devil that is contrary to the life that you have ordained for my children to lead on earth in the name of Jesus.

Gracious Father, you have said in your word that your will be done on the earth as it is done in heaven. And it isn't your will for the lives of my children for them to struggle under the attack of the enemy. I pray for the enforcement of your perfect will for the lives of my children right now in Jesus name.

Thank You Holy Father for hearing me in Jesus name.

**Prayers that Break Generational Curses**

Generational curses are transferable curses handed down from one generation to another within the same family. Once a child is born into any family with a generational curse, by the birth of that child in that family he will have a share in that curse that runs in that lineage. Which is the reason why you will see certain patterns that are common in some families it could be failure, infirmity, death, et cetera. One way to recognise the generational curses in any family is to look at the life of all its members. Father may suffer the same consequences, mother, sisters, uncles, brothers, cousins, and even distant relatives. Something is common among all of them. That is a generational curse that can also be broken in the Courts of heaven. That is what we are going to be doing right now for your children so that what affected your father, mother, sisters or grandparents would never have any effect on the lives of your children.

**Reflection**

Ezekiel 18:19-20

> *Yet say ye, Why? doth not the son bear the iniquity of the father? When the son hath done that which is lawful and right, and hath kept all my statutes, and*

> *hath done them, he shall surely live.*
> *20 The soul that sinneth, it shall die. The son shall not bear the iniquity of the father, neither shall the father bear the iniquity of the son: the righteousness of the righteous shall be upon him, and the wickedness of the wicked shall be upon him.*

Deuteronomy 24:16

> *16 The fathers shall not be put to death for the children, neither shall the children be put to death for the fathers: every man shall be put to death for his own sin.*

Holy Father, whatever generational curse that is running in my family is broken right now in the name of Jesus.

Heavenly Father, you have said in your word that thus far have you gone and no further will you go. I shield my children from any generational curse that has been attacking all the members of my family in the name of Jesus.

Holy Father, I come before you today to make this petition before your courts and to present this generational curse (mention the particular generational curse that you have identified in your family). You have said in your word that righteousness and justice are the foundation of your throne. I know that by the standard of your word it is not possible for my children to experience what I have experienced, to experience what other members of our family have experienced. Therefore, let that generational curse be broken over their lives and destiny in the name of Jesus.

Righteous Father, if the generational curse has been running in the lives of our family as a result of the covenant that was entered into by any member of our family in time past, I want you to judge by the standard of your word whether it is permissible for the fathers to eat sour graves and for the teeth of my children to be set on edge. If that is contrary to the standard of your word, then my children will never experience any generational curse in their lives in the name of Jesus.

Holy Father, I stand before your courts and declare by the standard of your word that the blood of Jesus speaks better things than the blood of Abel. May that same blood of Jesus speaks complete deliverance and liberation for my children from every effect of generational curse in the name of Jesus.

Gracious Father, I pray before your courts that this generational curse has ended by the authority in the name of Jesus.

Heavenly Father, from today (mention the particular generational curse that is rampant in your family) will become history in the name of Jesus.

Holy Father, as the power of the generational curse has been broken over the life of my children they are free from now and forever in the name of Jesus.

Thank you Holy Father for hearing me in Jesus name.

**Prayers for their Hedge**

The hedge of God upon the life of your children is one of the best defensive systems they can ever have in the world. As long as the hedge of God was upon the life of Job and his family, the devil couldn't touch them.

Job 1:9-10

> *Then Satan answered the Lord, and said, Doth Job fear God for nought?*
> *10 Hast not thou made an hedge about him, and about*

> *his house, and about all that he hath on every side? thou hast blessed the work of his hands, and his substance is increased in the land.*

So if your children can carry the hedge of God upon their lives, they will simply be untouchable to the kingdom of darkness. The devil has to go and seek special permission from God before he could attack the life of Job. Isn't this an interesting defence system that your children should have on the earth? Certainly, yes!

**Reflection**

Zechariah 2:5

> *For I, saith the Lord, will be unto her a wall of fire round about, and will be the glory in the midst of her.*

Psalms 125:2

> *As the mountains are round about Jerusalem, so the Lord is round about his people from henceforth even for ever.*

Holy Father, I pray that let the hedge of protection be upon my children forever in the name of Jesus.

Righteous Father, anything that my children can do which has the capacity of compromising their hedge, I pray that you help them to stay away from that thing in the name of Jesus.

Heavenly Father, you have said in your word that he that breaks the hedge, the serpent will bite. Release upon my children the grace not to break their hedge in the name of Jesus.

Righteous Father, let the blood of Jesus that speaks better things than the blood of Abel become a hedge upon the lives of my children in the name of Jesus.

Holy Father, may this hedge that you have placed upon the life of my children shield them from every arrow of the enemy in the name of Jesus.

Gracious Father, we have seen from your word that because of the hedge that was upon the life of Job the enemy couldn't touch him. May this hedge of protection upon the life of my children make them untouchable to the kingdom of darkness in the name of Jesus.

Thank you Holy Father because my prayers are answered in the name of Jesus.

**Prayers for their Purpose**

Do you know the purpose for which your child was sent to the earth? If you know the purpose for which your child was born or you got to know the purpose through a revelation from the Lord, you can use it before the courts of heaven and pray to frustrate all the agenda of darkness against the God-ordained destinies of your children. It is my prayer that the purpose for which God created your children will not fail in the name of Jesus.

**Reflection**

Jeremiah 29:11

> *For I know the thoughts that I think toward you, saith the Lord, thoughts of peace, and not of evil, to give you an expected end.*

Hebrews 13:6

> *So that we may boldly say, The Lord is my helper, and I will not fear what man shall do unto me.*

Holy Father, I come before your courts to plead my cause for the purpose of the creation of my children. I know that you have ordained this my child to become (mention the purpose for which your child was created to fulfil). I pray that let that purpose be accomplished in the life of my children in the name of Jesus.

Heavenly Father, you have said in your word that he that begun this good work will finish it. You have started this work in the life of my children, I ask that you help them to complete it and fulfil their destiny in the name of Jesus.

Glorious Father, whatever trap that the enemy has set in the future against my children to prevent them from fulfilling their God-ordained destinies, that trap is consumed by fire in the name of Jesus.

Holy Father, I pray for my children today that your will be done in their lives in the name of Jesus.

Righteous Father, whatever my children are capable of doing that has the potential of aborting the destiny you have prepared for them, show them your mercy so that they don't do those things in the name of Jesus.

Thank you, Lord for hearing and answering me in Jesus name.

## Restraining Orders and Injunctions in the courts of Heaven

### Reflection

Mark 9:25

> *When Jesus saw that the people came running together, he rebuked the foul spirit, saying unto him, Thou dumb and deaf spirit, I charge thee, come out of him, and enter no more into him.*

1 Samuel 7:13

> *So the Philistines were subdued, and they came no more into the coast of Israel: and the hand of the Lord was against the Philistines all the days of Samuel.*

Holy Father, I restrain all satanic arrows that have been planned against the life of my children in the name of Jesus.

Heavenly Father, I ask for the issuing of a permanent restraining order against all the arrows of Satan that he wants to use so that my children will miss it in their marital destiny in the name of Jesus.

Gracious Father, every spirit of failure at the edge of breakthrough that the enemy wants to use against the life of my children, it is restrained by the blood of Jesus.

Righteous Father, every limitation that the enemy has placed against the life of my children that limitation is forbidden from ever gaining expression in their lives in the name of Jesus.

Holy Father, you have said in your word that my children shall be the head and not the tail. Every smallness that the enemy intends to use against the life of my children, it is restrained by the blood of Jesus.

Gracious Father, I restrain every spirit of stubbornness that the enemy has fired into the lives of my children from manifesting in their lives in the name of Jesus.

Holy Father, I stand before your glorious courts and plead that every Delilah that the devil has prepared against the marital destinies of my children is restrained from finding them in the name of Jesus.

Heavenly Father, every planned death meant to abort the glorious life of my children before their due time on the earth, that death is restrained by the authority in the name of Jesus.

Righteous Father, every conspiracy prepared for my children to make them get into trouble in life, today the conspirators be they physical or spiritual, are restrained in Jesus name.

Holy Father, I plead the word cause of my children because you have said in your word that children are a heritage from the Lord and happy is the man that has his quiver full of them. Any spirit that wants to make my children become the source of pains and sorrow to my life stands restrained permanently in the name of Jesus.

## Prayers for releasing the Captive

If your child or any of your children is currently in prison, it is time for you to pray this prayer in the Courts of Heaven.

## Reflection

Psalms 86:15

> *But thou, O Lord, art a God full of compassion, and gracious, longsuffering, and plenteous in mercy and truth.*

Psalms 89:14

> *Justice and judgment are the habitation of thy throne: mercy and truth shall go before thy face.*

Holy Father, I thank you for the privilege that you have given to me to come before your courts at this hour. I am not taking it for granted Lord. I know that what my child has done is wrong. I also know that by the justice system of heaven, he deserved to be punished. I also know that by the justice system of the earth, he has fallen on the wrong side of the law. I did not come before your courts to justify his action. Lord, he was in the wrong and I acknowledge that before your courts. However, Lord, you are the God that can show mercy on whoever that you decide to show mercy, and compassion on whomever you choose. Holy Father, I pray that you will show mercy to my child who is currently in (mention the name of the prison where your child is currently being held) to be released from there in the name of Jesus.

Heavenly Father, you have said in your word that the heart of Kings is in the hand of the Lord and you turn it in whatever direction you desire. Whoever that is responsible for facilitating the release of my child from (mention the detention facility), I ask that in your mercy you will speak to the heart of the person or persons who are responsible for effecting his release in the name of Jesus.

The next set of prayer is for those who are detained for an unjustifiable cause in prison.

Holy Father, you have said in your word that righteousness and justice are the foundation of your throne. And several times in the Holy Scriptures, you have warned people not to be unjust. My children have been jailed for what they did not do. Holy Father, I know that this is unjust by your standard. I, therefore, ask that you cause them to be released in the name of Jesus.

Righteous Father, whoever that is responsible for the conspiracy of my children being sent to prison, I ask that you cause the person to go and confess the truth before the authorities that will lead to the release of my child/children from prison in the name of Jesus.

Thank you holy father because you have heard and answered all of my prayers concerning my child/children to you be all the glory and the honour in the name of Jesus.

## Important Decision

If you are reading this book and you are not saved, pray this prayer after me:

Lord Jesus, I come before you today. I give you my heart. I give you my all. Come into my life. Become my Lord and saviour. Deliver me from the power of sin. Help me to live for you forever, in Jesus name.

## Free Gift

Get these Four Powerful Books for Free and Revolutionize Your Christian Life

**Grant Me Access**

**Prayer**

Let us know about your prayer needs as our team add you to our prayer list and intercede fervently on your behalf.

Also, check our blog for Holy Ghost inspired content.

www.thetentofglory.com

I would love to hear from you how our ministry and our books have blessed you. Write to us at

pius@thetentofglory.com

## More Reading

Our Books

1. Operating in the Angelic Realm: Prayers that Activate the Ministry of Angels

2. Prayers that Delete Spiritual Marks: Powerful Prayers for Complete Deliverance from Spiritual Marks and Breakthroughs

3. The Courts of Heaven: Prayers that Open the Courts of Heaven for Healing and Deliverance

4. Courtroom Prayers that Destroy Witchcraft: Courts of Heaven Prayer to Break Witchcraft Attacks

5. Breaking Financial Hardship in the Courts of Heaven: Courts of Heaven Prayers That Destroy Financial Bondage and Yokes

6. Psalm 23: The Power of the 23rd Psalm, the Lord is my Shepherd and Your Provisions

7. Courtroom Prayers for Beginners: A Complete Guide to Courts of Heaven Prayers

8. 7 Powerful Prayers of Friendship with the Holy Spirit

9. Restraining Decrees through Courtroom Prayers: Courts of Heaven Orders for Victory & Breakthroughs

10. Python Spirit: Complete Deliverance from the Python Spirit with Powerful Prayers

11. Powerful Prayers for Your Adult Children: How to Pray for Your Children and Secure their Future

12. Praying for My Future Husband: How to Pray for Your Husband and Enjoy A Godly Marriage

13. Prayers That Bring You Closer to the Holy Spirit: Powerful Prayers, Intense Reflection to Become the Closest Friend of the Holy Ghost (Holy Ghost Friendship Guide Book 3)

14. Praying God's Promises to Reality: Simple Ways of Praying the Promises of God for Victory & Breakthrough

15. God Wants You Protected From Disease

16. Under His Divine Protection

17. 7 Day Fasting Challenge That Will Change Your Life Forever: 7 Powerful Prayers to Pray in 7 Days

18. Praying Through the Book of Psalms for Financial Miracle: The Financial Miracle Prayer for Breakthrough

19. Burning Evil Garments: Prayers That Destroy Evil Garments, Deliverance, Breakthroughs And God's Favour Into Your Life

20. 30 Days with the Holy Spirit: Powerful Prayers and Devotional for Personal Connection with the Holy Spirit and Be His Friend

21. Breaking Evil Altars: Prayers, Decrees, Declarations for Dismantling Evil Altars

22. How to see the Supernatural: Powerful Prayers that open the Unseen Realm

23. Breaking the Spell of Disfavour: Prayers Declarations and Decrees

24. Deliverance from Shame and Reproach: Prayers, Declarations for Victory

25. Prayers that Destroy Infirmities & Diseases: Powerful Prayers that bring Healing to the Sick

26. Courtroom Prayers: Prayers And Declarations in the Courts of Heaven For Victory, Breakthrough, and Deliverance

27. How to make the Holy Ghost Your Closest Friend (Book 2)

28. The Keys to Fervent Prayer: The Prayer Warrior Guide to Praying Always

29. Interpretation of Tongues: Be Filled with the Spirit, Unlock Speaking in Tongues & Know What You Are Praying

30. Deliverance from negative Dreams and Nightmares by Force

31. How to Build a Life of Personal Devotion to God (Free-Ebook)

32. The Holy Spirit Friendship Manual: How to make the Holy Ghost Your Close Friend (Free-Ebook)

33. Walking in the Path of Divine Direction Always

34. The Expediency of Tongues

35. Breaking Soul Ties the Simple Way: How to Break Soul Ties and Receive Freedom

36. How to Read the Bible And Understand It

37. BAPTISM OF THE HOLY SPIRIT: Easy Steps to be Filled With the Holy Spirit And Obtain the Gifts of the Holy Spirit

38. Prayer That Never Fails

39. Vision from The Heavenly

40. Baptism of the Holy Ghost Prayer Book: How to Minister the Baptism of the Holy Ghost to yourself and others.

41. How to Hear God's Voice: A Believer's Manual For Talking with God

42. Guide to Effective Fasting and Praying: A Way of Fasting And Prayers That Guarantee Results

# Courts of Heaven Prayers for Your Children

Pius Joseph

Courts of Heaven Prayers for Your Children

Printed in Great Britain
by Amazon